PITTSBURG

Horses

ALICE TWINE

PowerKiDS press

For Ali Tracey

Published in 2008 by The Rosen Publishing Group, Inc.
29 East 21st Street, New York, NY 10010

First Edition

Editor: Amelie von Zumbusch
Book Design: Julio Gil
Photo Researcher: Nicole Pristash

Photo Credits: Cover, p. 1 Darin Epperly/Getty Images; pp. 5, 7, 9, 11, 15, 17, 19, 21, 23, 24 (top left, top right, bottom left) © www.shutterstock.com; pp. 13, 24 (bottom right) © www.istockphoto.com/Markanja.

Library of Congress Cataloging-in-Publication Data

Twine, Alice.
  Horses / Alice Twine. — 1st ed.
      p. cm. — (Baby animals)
  Includes index.
  ISBN-13: 978-1-4042-3774-2 (library binding) ISBN-10: 1-4042-3774-7 (library binding)
  1. Foals—Juvenile literature. I. Title.
  SF302.T85 2008
  636.1—dc22
                                        2006038114

Manufactured in the United States of America.

Contents

Baby horses are called foals. A male foal is known as a colt. A female foal is called a filly.

A foal is born with a tail and a **mane**. As the foal grows older, its tail and mane will grow longer.

Foals come in different colors. This is a **bay** foal. Bay foals have brown coats, black manes, and black tails.

There are many kinds, or breeds, of horses. This foal is a quarter horse. Quarter horses are fast runners.

Baby **ponies**, like these Dartmoor ponies, are also called foals. Ponies are smaller than horses. Ponies have thick coats and tails.

This is a **newborn** foal. Foals learn to walk just a few hours after they are born.

15

Newborn foals drink their mother's milk. After a few weeks, foals start to eat grass, just as adult horses do.

17

Grown-up horses sleep standing up, but foals sleep lying down. Foals sleep a lot.

19

Foals also play a lot. They like to run and jump.

Foals grow up to become strong, fast horses. Young horses can run as fast as 50 miles per hour (80 km/h).

23

Words to Know

bay

mane

newborn

ponies

Web Sites

Due to the changing nature of Internet links, PowerKids Press has developed an online list of Web sites related to the subject of this book. This site is updated regularly. Please use this link to access the list: www.powerkidslinks.com/baby/horses/